MASTER THE UKULELE 2

ISBN-13: **978-1-7359692-99**
UKELIKETHEPROS.COM
© 2022 TERRY CARTER

TABLE OF CONTENTS

MASTER THE UKULELE 2

Master The Ukulele 2 by Uke Like The Pros is the long awaited follow-up to best-selling book and ukulele course, Master The Ukulele 1. Master The Ukulele 2 by Terry Carter takes what you learned in Master The Ukulele 1 and blasts those skills and techniques to the moon. The Master The Ukulele 2 book offers a step-by-step approach to learning and mastering the ukulele for the Intermediate ukulele player. With this book you get free access to the Master The Ukulele 2 backing tracks for every lesson at *ukelikethepros.com/master-2.*

Master The Ukulele 2 is broken up into 2 sections, plus an added twist. In the 1st section you will learn the most popular songs, chords, chord progressions, and strum patterns, for all ukulele players. You will dive deep into Rock, Pop, Island, Reggae, and Jazz styles. You will take your knowledge of chords and strumming to levels you can't imagine by learning songs in the style of classic songs such as Stand By Me, Stir It Up, Santeria, Creep, Knockin' On Heaven's Door, Blvd. of Broken Dreams, With or Without You, Island In The Sun, Can't Help

Falling In Love, What A Wonderful World, and Honky-Tonk Woman. There is no better way to learn and improve your ukulele playing than by mastering songs in the style of greats such as IZ, Bob Marley, Radiohead, Sublime, Green Day, Bob Dylan, Elvis, 21 Pilots, The Rolling Stones, Weezer, Louis Armstrong, Ben E. King, and U2. In the second section you dig hard into the Blues. Although you learned a lot of Blues and scales in Master The Ukulele 1, your Blues playing will go even further in Master the Ukulele 2. You will learn Shuffle Blues, Blues Rock, Jump Blues, Country Blues, Strumming Blues, Single-Note Blues, Minor Blues, Jazz Blues, Chuck Berry Blues, Octave Blues, and even a Blues Solo. You will master the Blues in many keys by studying the styles of Blues greats such as Chuck Berry, B.B. King, Muddy Waters, T-Bone Water, Stevie-Ray Vaughan, Johnny Cash, Wes Montgomery, Robert Johnson, and Jimi Hendrix.

The twist of the book is that besides mastering Classic Songs and Blues, you will learn how to fingerpick with House Of The Rising Sun, study Classical music with Ode To Joy by Beethoven, learn

TAB, understand Beginning and Advanced Strum Patterns, and learn how to play a complete Blues solo using the Blues Scale. Terry Carter is a master musician and teacher who has spent over 30 years as a studio musician, producer, and writer, working with greats such as Weezer, Josh Groban, Robby Krieger (The Doors), 2-time Grammy-winning composer Christopher Tin (Calling All Dawns), Duff McKagan (Guns N' Roses), Grammy-winning producer Charles Goodan (Santana/Rolling Stones), and the Los Angeles Philharmonic.

Terry has written and produced tracks for commercials (Discount Tire and Puma) and TV shows, including Scorpion (CBS), Pit Bulls & Parolees (Animal Planet), Trippin', Wildboyz, and The Real World (MTV). He has published more than 15 books for Uke Like The Pros and Rock Like The Pros, filmed over 30 ukulele and guitar online courses, and has millions of views on his social media channels.

Terry received a Master of Music in Studio/Jazz Guitar Performance from University of Southern California, and a Bachelor of Music from San Diego State University, with an emphasis in Jazz Studies and Music Education. He has taught at the University of Southern California, San Diego State University, Santa Monica College, Miracosta College, and Los Angeles Trade Tech College.

Sounds Good?

It's now your turn to dive into the *Master the Ukulele 2 Book.*

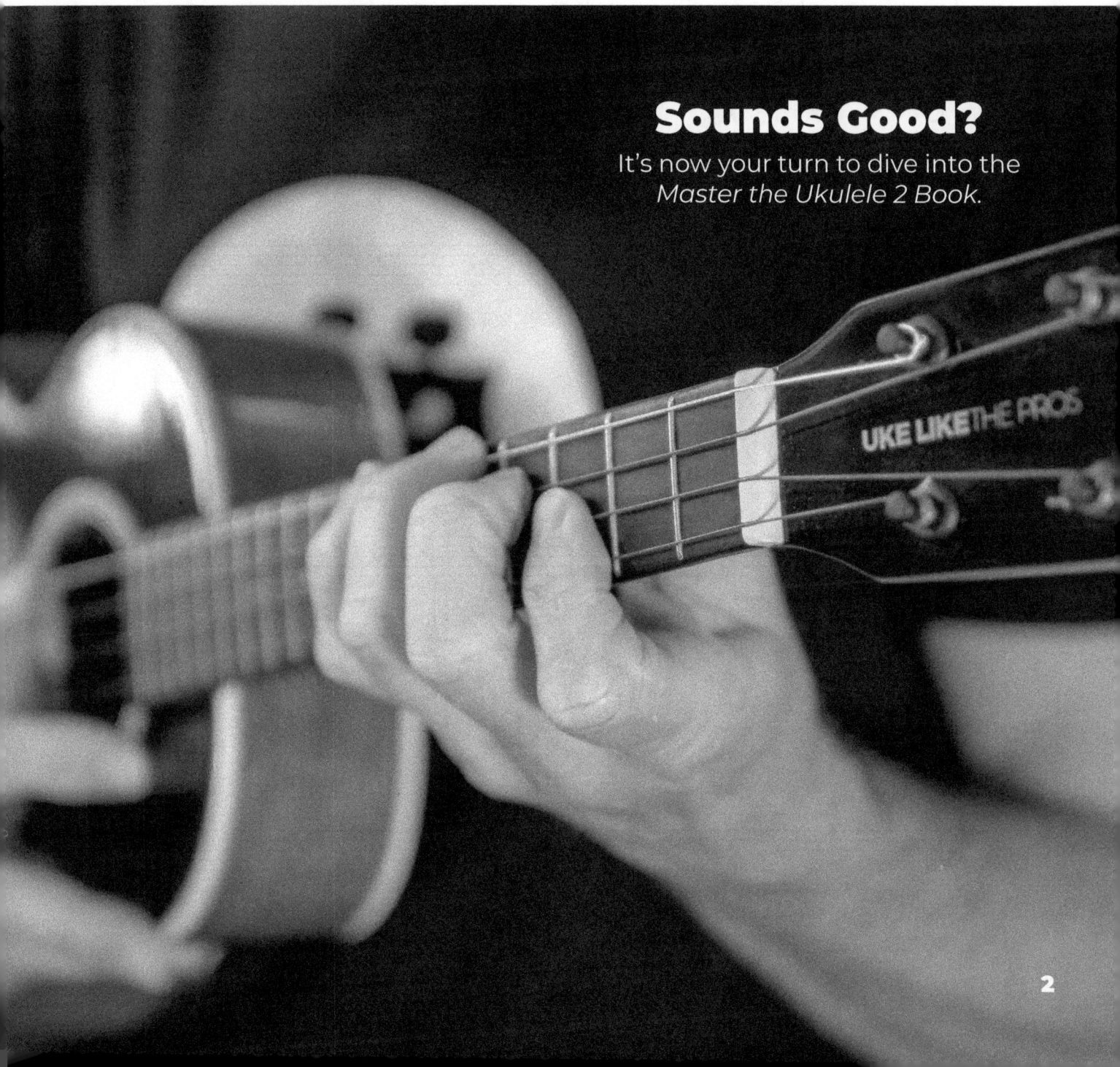

HEAVEN'S GATE
(In the Style of **Knockin' On Heaven's Door**)

This song uses the "G," "D," "Amin," and "C" chords. There are 4 different strum patterns you can use depending on your level of playing, with a final goal of playing the sixteenth note pattern in the chorus. Remember that changing strum patterns during a song helps bring variety and keeps your audience's attention.

Folk Rock

♩=60

Intro

Verse

Chorus

To Verse

SHATTERED HOPES
(In the Style of **Blvd Of Broken Dreams**)

This song has 3 different strum patterns, and uses both open position chords and bar chords. The Introduction starts off with Down Down-Up quarter and eighth notes, then builds into a busier sixteenth-note pattern for the Verse, and then rocks out during the Chorus using all downstroke eighth notes.

TWIST OF FATE
(In the Style of **With Or Without You** - KEY OF C MAJOR)

This progression "C," "G," "Amin," "F" (or I-V-vi-IV) is the most widely used progression in music. It uses all basic open-position chords and the "Island Strum," or the "Grandaddy Strum" pattern. To master this strum pattern, pay attention to the tie between the "+" of "2" and beat "3." The tie means to hold so you won't strum on beat "3."

Key of C Major

TWIST OF FATE
(In the Style of **With Or Without You** - KEY OF D MAJOR)

This is the same chord progression, I-V-vi-IV, but moved up a whole step to the key of D. In the key of D, the chords are "D," "A," "Bmin," and "G." These are all open position chords except the "Bmin," which is a bar chord. Use the "Island Strum" for this one.

Key of D Major

TUMBLE & FALL
(In the Style of **Stand By Me**)

This song is in the key of A, and uses the "A," "F#min," "D," and "E" chords. The strum pattern is the "Island Strum," but it has a mute (X) on beat 2. To mute, place the palm of your strumming hand on all the strings over the sound-hole right before you strike the strings, so it produces a "muffled" sound.

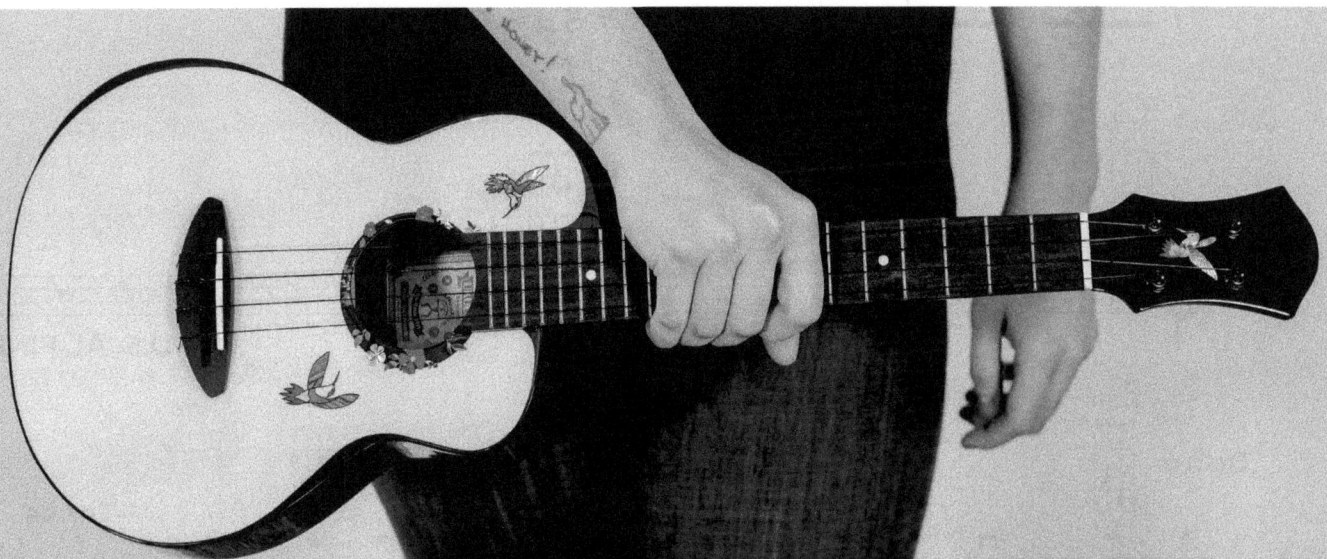

MASTER THE UKULELE 2 VIDEO COURSE
UKELIKETHEPROS.COM

6

HIP HIP
(In the Style of **Island In The Sun**)

Are you ready to rock? This song will use several different strum patterns, and both open position and power chords. Power chords are 2-note chords that give you a rock sound. The strum pattern, in the intro, verse, and outro, is tricky because it uses mutes on beat 2 and 4, and also switches chords on the up (v) strums. The chorus uses all down-stroke eighth notes with the power chords.

GIMME GIMME
(In the Style of **Honky Tonk Woman**)

This progression has some mutes (X) in it to give it a country-rock sound. Since some of the mutes are on up strokes you have to use both your chord and strumming hand to mute the strings. It also takes your basic C and D chords, and adds the "sus 4" to them, used by greats such as Keith Richards, Jimmy Page, and Pete Townsend.

FOOLS RUSH IN
(In the Style of Can't Help Falling In Love)

This classic progression has a contemporary sixteenth-note strum pattern, with quarter notes on beats 1 and 3, and sixteenth notes on beats 2 and 4. There are a lot of different chords in this progression, including the "C," "Emin," "Amin," "F," "G," "B7," and "A7."

ALL YOUR MUSIC NEEDS

SKIES OF BLUE

(In the Style of **What A Wonderful World**)

The chord progression from this song is one of the all-time great ukulele progressions heard by such greats as IZ and Louis Armstrong. It uses a sixteenth-note strum pattern, and lots of jazz chords, including the seventh, augmented, diminished, minor 7(b5), 7(b9), and minor 6 chords.

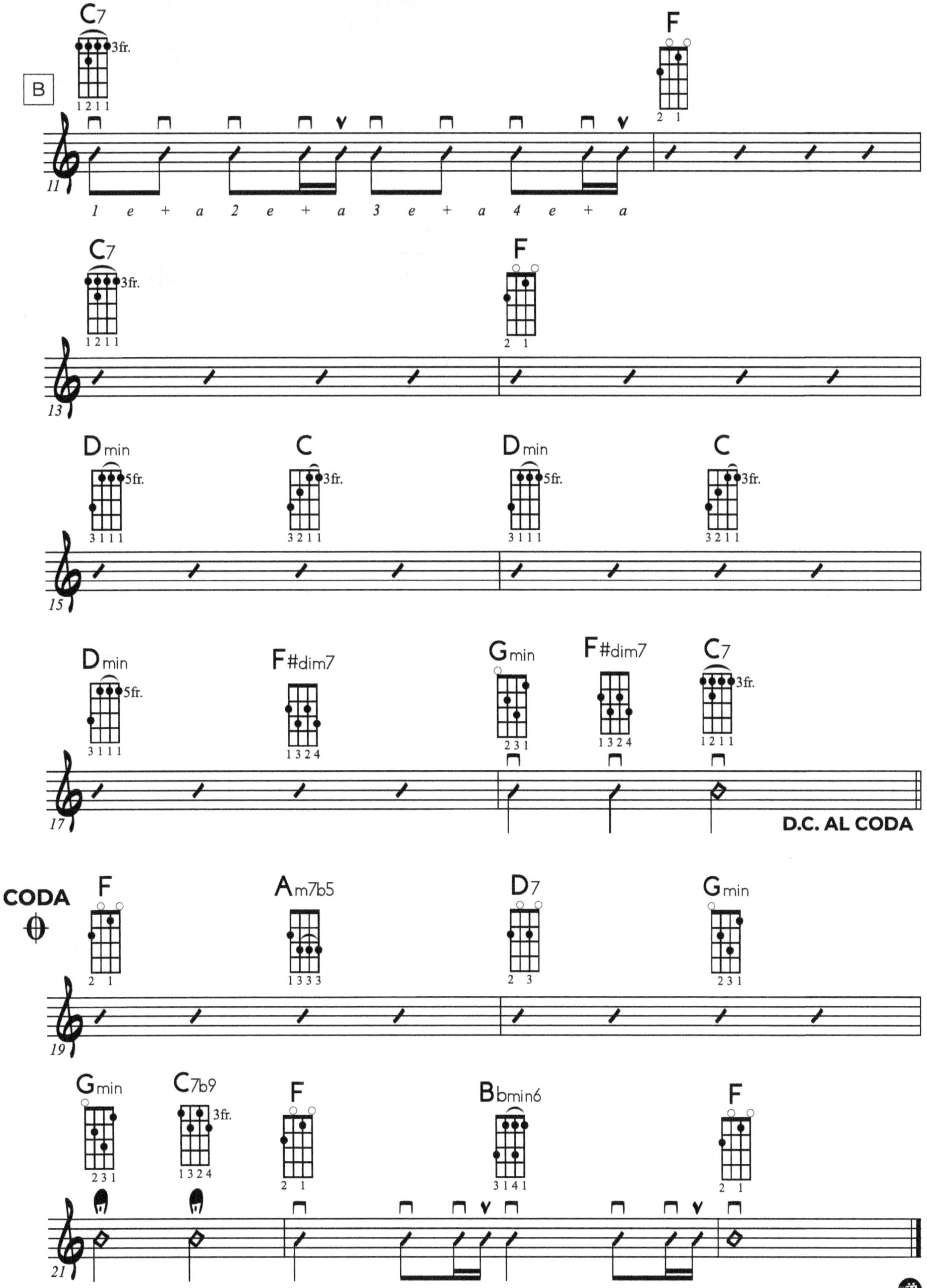
B
C7
3fr.
1 2 1 1
F
2 1
11
1 e + a 2 e + a 3 e + a 4 e + a
C7
3fr.
1 2 1 1
F
2 1
13
Dmin
5fr.
3 1 1 1
C
3fr.
3 2 1 1
Dmin
5fr.
3 1 1 1
C
3fr.
3 2 1 1
15
Dmin
5fr.
3 1 1 1
F#dim7
1 3 2 4
Gmin
2 3 1
F#dim7
1 3 2 4
C7
3fr.
1 2 1 1
17
D.C. AL CODA
CODA
F
2 1
Am7b5
1 3 3 3
D7
2 3
Gmin
2 3 1
19
Gmin
2 3 1
C7b9
3fr.
1 3 2 4
F
2 1
Bbmin6
3 1 4 1
F
2 1
21

MOTEL SIX
(In the Style of **1977 Classic Rock**)

In this great progression, we twist and turn through minor, major, and seventh chords. It uses one of the coolest, but most complex sixteenth-note strum patterns you'll play with "+" between the "a" of beat 2 and beat 3.

RUN AWAY
(In the Style of **Creep**)

The challenging parts of this progression are the bar chords, the strum pattern, and the repetition. You will be challenged with the "B," "C," and "C minor" bar chords, as well as the sixteenth-note strum pattern, which is similar to the one we saw our previous song.

Rock

♩=92

Verse/Chorus

G   B

C   Cmin   G

1 e + a 2 e + a 3 e + a 4 e + a   **Sim...**

4 Times

MIX THE POT
(In the Style of **Stir It Up**)

The main characteristic of this Reggae ukulele style is playing a sixteenth-note "down-up" strum pattern on the off beats (playing in between, but not on beats 1, 2, 3, or 4). Reggae style also uses three-note chords played on the higher strings and frets of the ukulele.

SANCHO'S REVENGE
(In the Style of **Santeria**)

This Reggae rhythm style is different than the previous one because you only play eighth-note "upstrokes" on the off beats. You will play the "E," "Ab," "Dbmin," and "B" chords using three-note shapes played up the fretboard of the ukulele.

ODE TO JOY

Let's change gears in this song, and only focus on single notes. In this classic Beethoven song, you can either read the notation or the TAB. Although this song seems long and complex, the A, B, and D sections are very similar. Take the C section slow, as it does jump around the strings.

♩=128

By Ludwig Van Beethoven

A

Counting: 1 + 2 + 3 + 4 + 1 + 2 + 3 + 4 + 1 + 2 + 3 + 4 + 1 + 2 + 3 + 4 +

Fingering: 1 3 3 1 2 2 2 2

B

1 + 2 + 3 + 4 + 1 + 2 + 3 + 4 + 1 + 2 + 3 + 4 + 1 + 2 + 3 + 4 +

1 3 3 1 2 2 2

C

1 + 2 + 3 + 4 + 1 + 2 + 3 + 4 + 1 + 2 + 3 + 4 + 1 + 2 + 3 + 4 +

2 2 2 1 2 1 2 2

D

1 + 2 + 3 + 4 + 1 + 2 + 3 + 4 + 1 + 2 + 3 + 4 + 1 + 2 + 3 + 4 +

1 3 3 1 2 2 2

HORIZON'S SUN

(In the Style of **House Of The Rising Sun**)

The rasgueado strum pattern used in this song is a very cool and challenging pattern to play. Once mastered, it can be used as an alternate strum-pattern to give your music a Spanish flamenco sound. Make sure to practice it slowly and get your technique right before speeding it up.

BLUES SHUFFLE IN G
(Quick Change)

This blues shuffle is in the key of G, and has a quick change. It is a 12-bar blues the typical I (G), IV (C), and V (D) chords and has a cool turnaround in measures 11-12. The quick change is when you go to the IV (C) chord in the second measure.

ROCKIN' BLUES IN G
(Quick Change)

This is a straight eighth-note blues in the key of G that has a quick change. It is a 12-bar blues using the I (G), IV (C), and V (D) chords, but the straight eighth notes give it more of a driving blues-rock feel and sound. Notice the quick change to the IV (C) chord in the second measure.

WALKING THE DOG BLUES
(In A)

This Blues Shuffle in A is a single note rhythm part. Once you learn the pattern for the A7 chord, the patterns for the D7 and E7 are similar except on different strings and frets. Start with all downstrokes and then try alternate picking (down, up, down up, etc.). There is a cool ½ step slide from the F7 to the E7 at the end.

Shuffle Blues

♩=84

OCTAVE JUMP BLUES
(In A)

This variation of our Straight eighth-note Blues in "A" is based on a repeating pattern that starts off with an "Octave" jump. An "Octave" is 2 notes of the same pitch that are eight diatonic notes apart, simply meaning the notes sound the same, but one is higher in pitch than the other.

Straight Blues

$\quad$ = 126

CHUCK BERRY STYLE BLUES
(In A)

This Blues Rock style in A uses "closed" position chords (no open strings) and straight eighth notes. The last 4 measures are different than many Blues because we only play the V (E) and I (A) chords. This is similar to what Chuck Berry, Jerry Lee Lewis, and Little Richard would play to get the driving blues/rock sound.

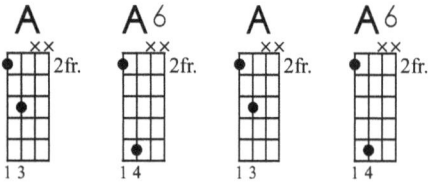

CHUCK BERRY STYLE BLUES
(In Bb)

This Blues Rock style in Bb uses "closed" position chords and straight eighth notes. This is exactly the same as our previous lesson, but is in Bb, which is ½ step or 1 fret higher than our previous lesson in the key of A.

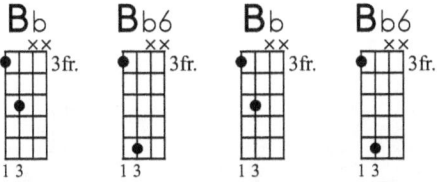

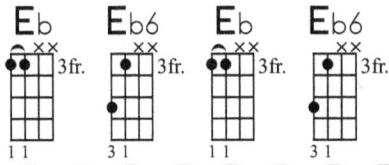

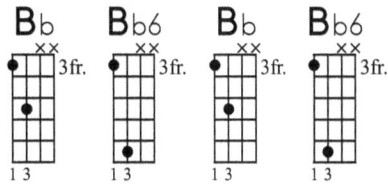

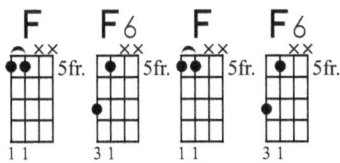

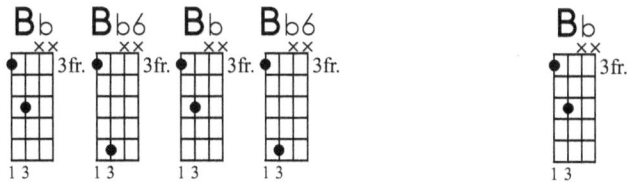

CHUCK BERRY STYLE BLUES SHUFFLE

(In Bb) PAGE 01 OF 02

This Blues Shuffle in Bb uses "closed" position chords and uses swing eighth notes. The shuffle feel helps give this one a more traditional Blues sound. Notice the cool and essential turnaround in the last 2 measures.

Swing Blues

♩=94

Counting: 1 + 2 + 3 + 4 + *Sim.*

Bb
Bb6
Bb
Bb6
3fr.
F
F6
F
F6
5fr.
Eb
Eb6
Eb
Eb6
3fr.
Bb
F#7
F7
Bb
Fingering:

JAZZ BLUES
(In C)

In this lesson we will explore the Jazz Blues in C. This Blues progression uses Dominant 7th chords, Minor 7th chords, a quick change, and the I-VI-ii-V turnaround. Make sure to follow the rest on beat 2 and stop the sound to give it an authentic Jazz rhythm sound.

ALL YOUR MUSIC NEEDS

TERRYCARTERMUSICSTORE.COM

COUNTRY BLUES

This lesson will help you get started playing a Country Blues feel. The technique involves playing bass notes with the thumb (p) on the downbeats "1," "2," "3," and "4," and chord strums in between with the 1st finger (i). The bass notes (root and 5th) alternate between the 4th and 3rd strings.

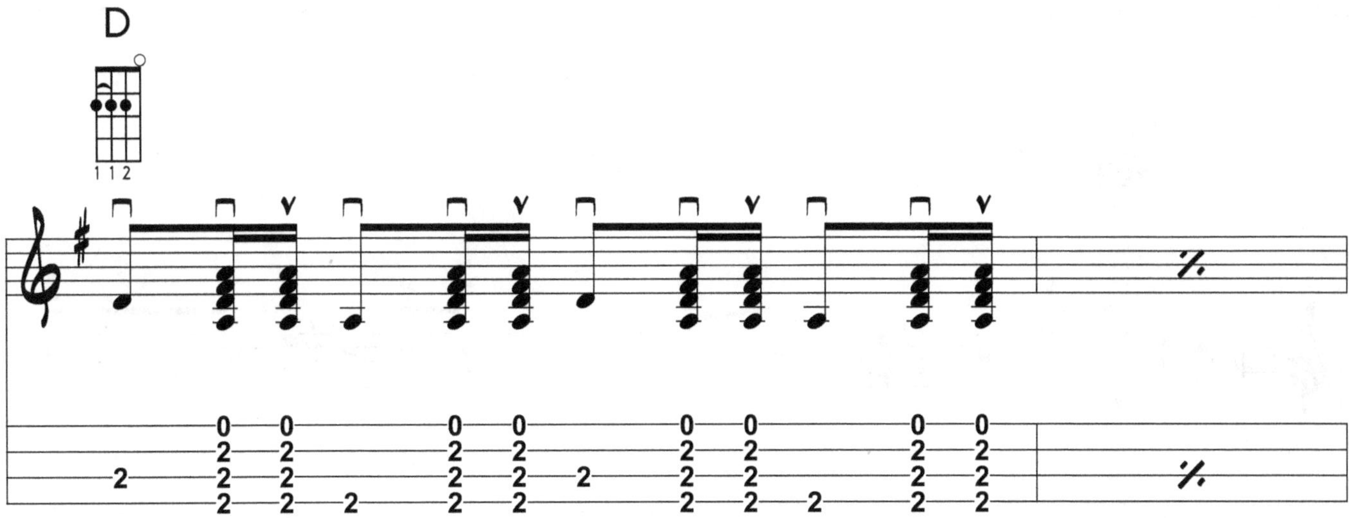
D
1 1 2

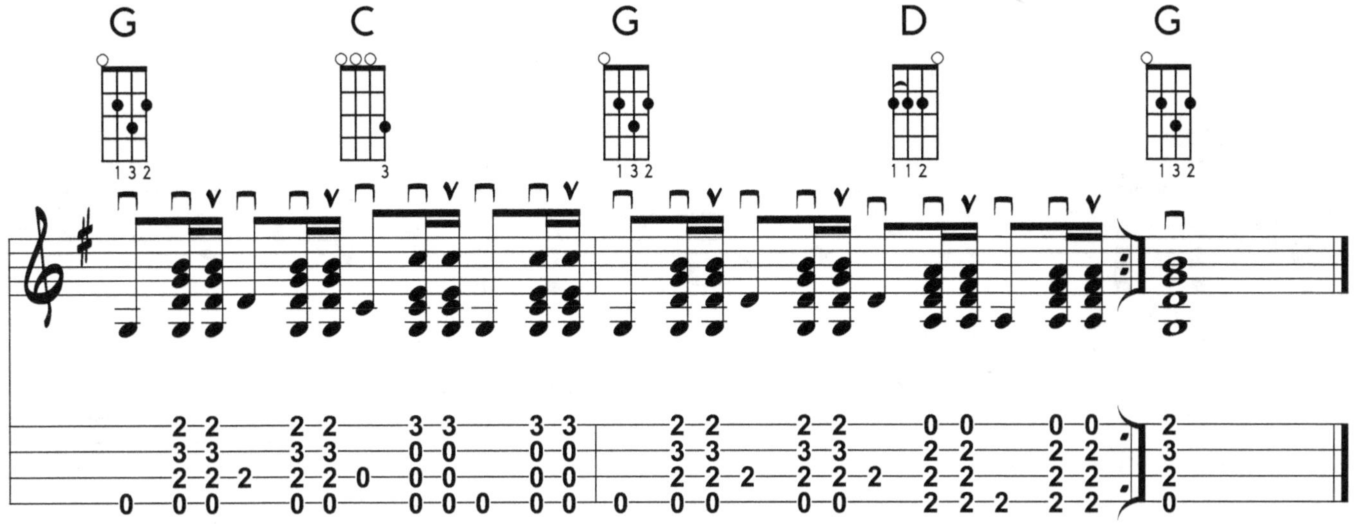
G
1 3 2
C
3
G
1 3 2
D
1 1 2
G
1 3 2

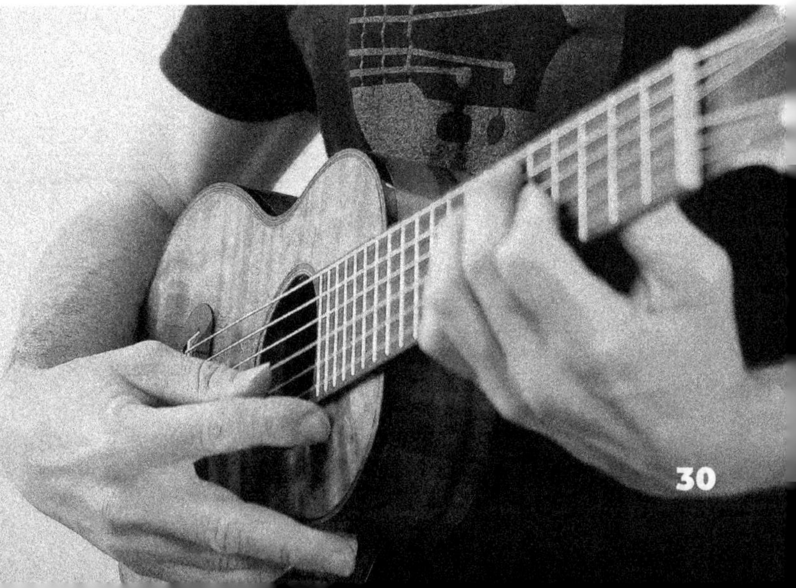

C MINOR SLOW BLUES

This Slow Minor Blues in C minor uses a combination of chords and single notes. The Minor Blues gives a darker sound, using chords like C Minor 7, F Minor, Ab7, G7, and G Augmented. This will work on using slides, hammer ons, and triplets.

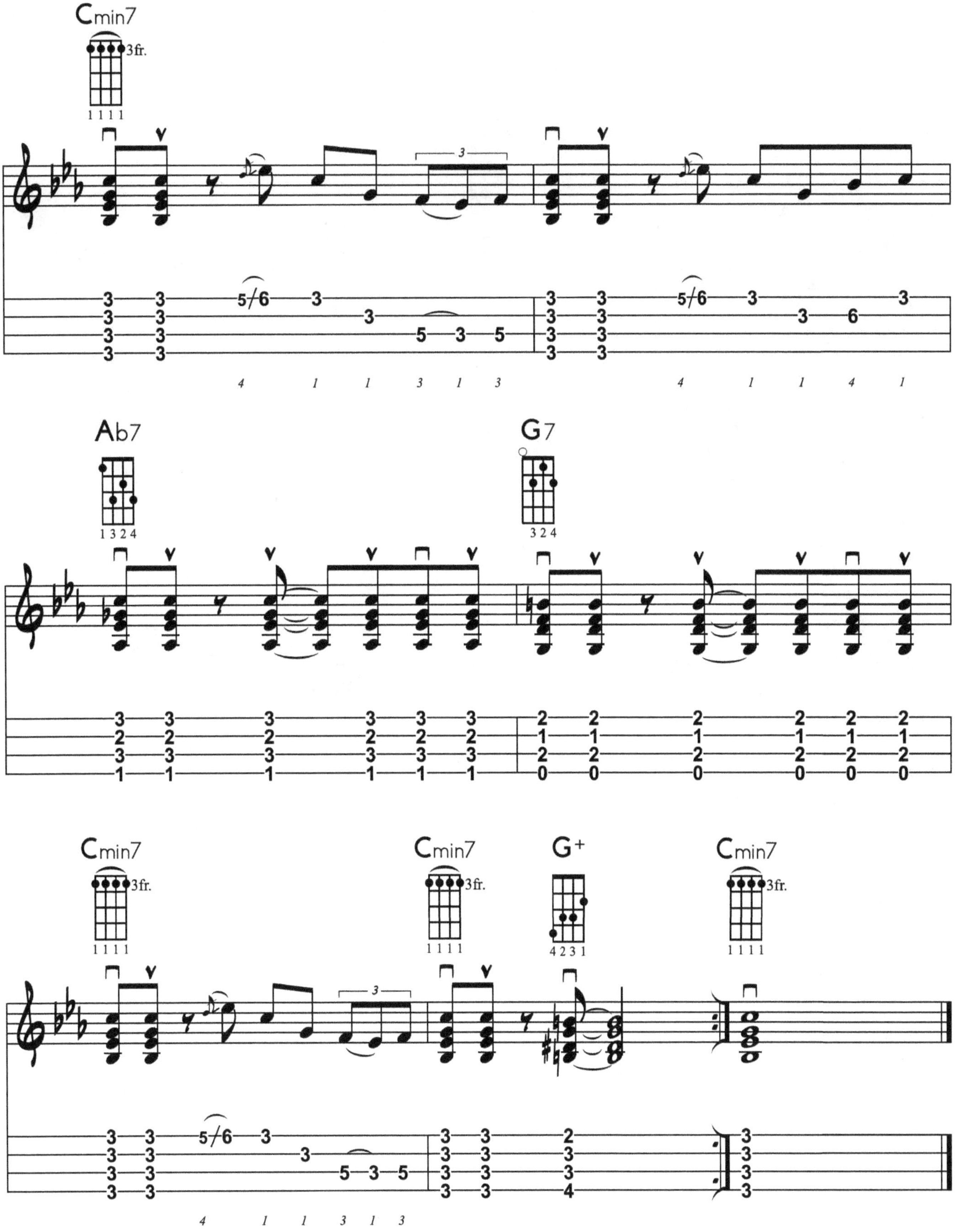
Cmin7
3fr.
Ab7
G7
Cmin7
Cmin7
G+
Cmin7

BLUES SOLO (In A)

This lesson works on playing a Blues solo using the A Minor Pentatonic Scale. You will learn how to take the scale, and break it up into smaller licks and riffs to make it sound like a melodic solo. Once mastered, you can take the scale and create your own licks and solo ideas.

ALL YOUR MUSIC NEEDS

GREAT JOB!

YOU DID IT! Congratulations, you completed the Master The Ukulele 2 book. I'm so proud of you for making the commitment to master the ukulele with this Uke Like The Pros book. Continue to use this book as a resource, and work on always improving your technique and confidence.

Did you have fun with these songs? Want to learn more ukulele?

Here at Uke Like The Pros, we love to teach the ukulele, and nothing brings us more joy than seeing you improve your playing. At ukelikethepros.com we have a step-by-step path for you to follow, so you know exactly which course will match your skill level. The next steps are the 23 Ultimate Chord Progressions course, the Beginning Ukulele Fingerstyle Songbook, the Beginning Ukulele Blues Mastery Course, or the Beginning Ukulele Music Reading Course.

If you want it all, you can join the Platinum Membership. The Platinum Membership gives you access to every course at **ukelikethepros.com**, including access to the member-only forum, weekly LIVE Q & A video calls, and VIP access to challenges and workshops. Check out the Platinum Membership at **ukelikethepros. com/platinum**.

I look forward to connecting with you more at **ukelikethepros.com**, and **terrycartermusicstore.com**, and all the UkeLikeThePros social media channels.

Talk soon,
Terry Carter.

THE ESSENTIALS

It is important to learn and memorize these terms and symbols because they not only apply to ukulele but to all music.

Treble Clef or "G" Clef | Staff

Time Signature

Measure Numbers

Measure or Bar

Bar Line | End

Top Number:
How Many Beats Per Measure

♩= 120 — Tempo Marks
120 bpm (beats per minute)

Bottom Number:
What Kind of Note Gets the Beat

Common Time:
Same as 4/4 Time

Repeat Sign

Notes On The Staff: There are seven notes in music (A, B, C, D, E, F, G) and they move up and down alphabetically on the staff.

G A B C D E F G A B C D E F G A B C D E F

How To Remember The Notes:

Notes On The Lines | Notes in The Spaces

E (every)   G (good)   B (boy)   D (does)   F (fine)   F   A   C   E

A

HOW TO READ TAB

Tablature (TAB) is a form of music reading for ukulele that uses a 4 line staff and numbers. Each line of the staff represents a string on the ukulele and the numbers represent which fret you play on. When looking at the TAB staff it reads like it's upside down on the paper compared to the strings of your ukulele. On the TAB staff, the highest line (closest to the sky) represents the 1st string (A string) of the ukulele, while the lowest line (closest to the ground) represents the 4th string (G string) of the ukulele. When you see 2 or more notes stacked on top of each other on the TAB staff, that means you play those notes at the same time, like a a chord.

UKULELE STRINGS

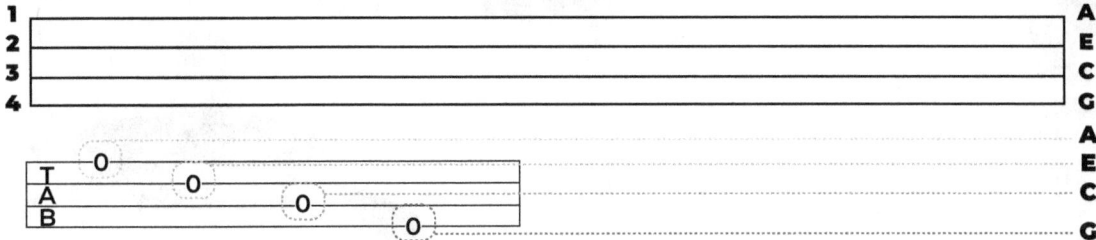

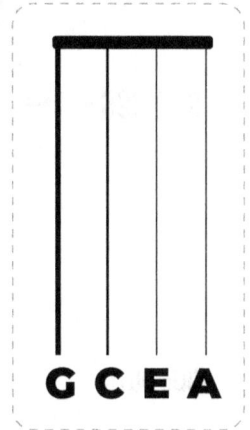

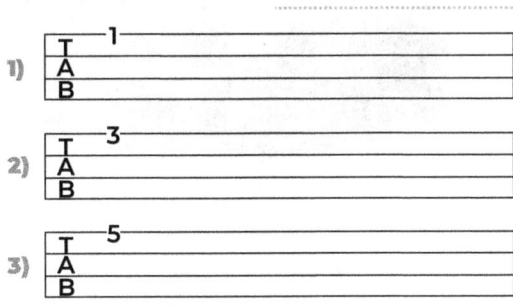

1rst STRING EXAMPLES

1) A string. FIRST FRET.
2) A string. THIRD FRET.
3) A string. FIFTH FRET.

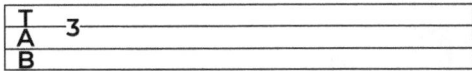

2nd STRING - E string. THIRD FRET.

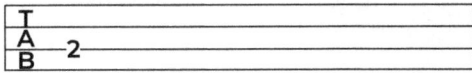

3rd STRING - C string. SECOND FRET.

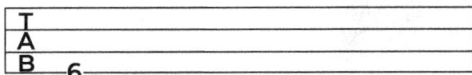

4th STRING - G string. SIXTH FRET.

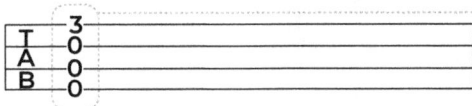

CHORD C

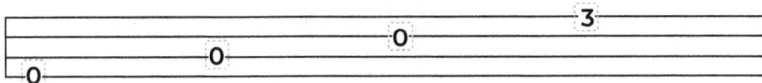

ARPEGGIO
USING THE C CHORD

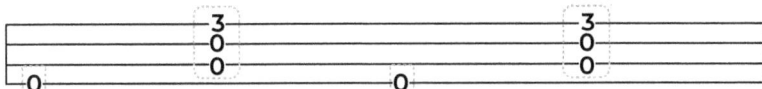

PINCH
USING THE C CHORD

UKULELE PARTS

HEADSTOCK

ULTP SIGNATURE

STRINGS

NUT

FRETS

SIDE DOTS

FRET MARKERS
ON FRETBOARD

SIDE

BODY

FRETBOARD

ROSETTE

SOUND HOLE

TOP

BRIDGE

TUNERS

SADDLE

NECK

BUTT

HEEL

BINDING

SIDE

BACK

UKULELE HANDS

When playing fingerstyle on your ukulele, you will see both letters and numbers to indicate which fingers to use both for picking hand and your fretting hand. These letters and numbers will show up in the music notation, TAB, and chord diagrams.

FRETTING HAND	PICKING HAND
The left hand for right-handed players. will be indicated in the music or chord diagrams by numbers: **1**=Index finger **3**=Ring finger **2**=Middle finger **4**=Pinky finger	The right hand for right-handed players. will be indicated in the music by letters: **p**=Thumb **m**=middle **i**=index **a**=ring **c**=pinky (not used in this course)

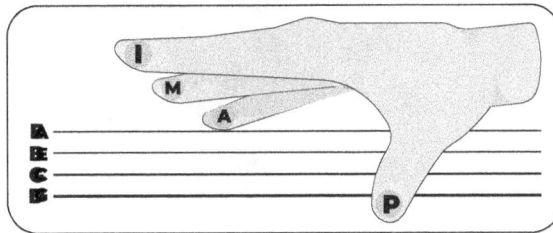

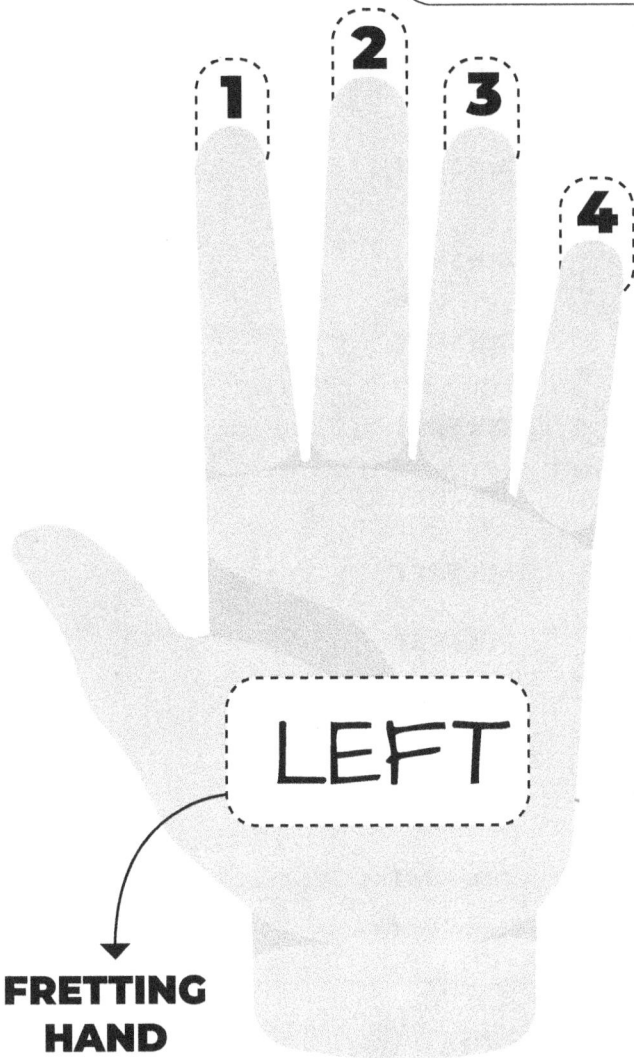

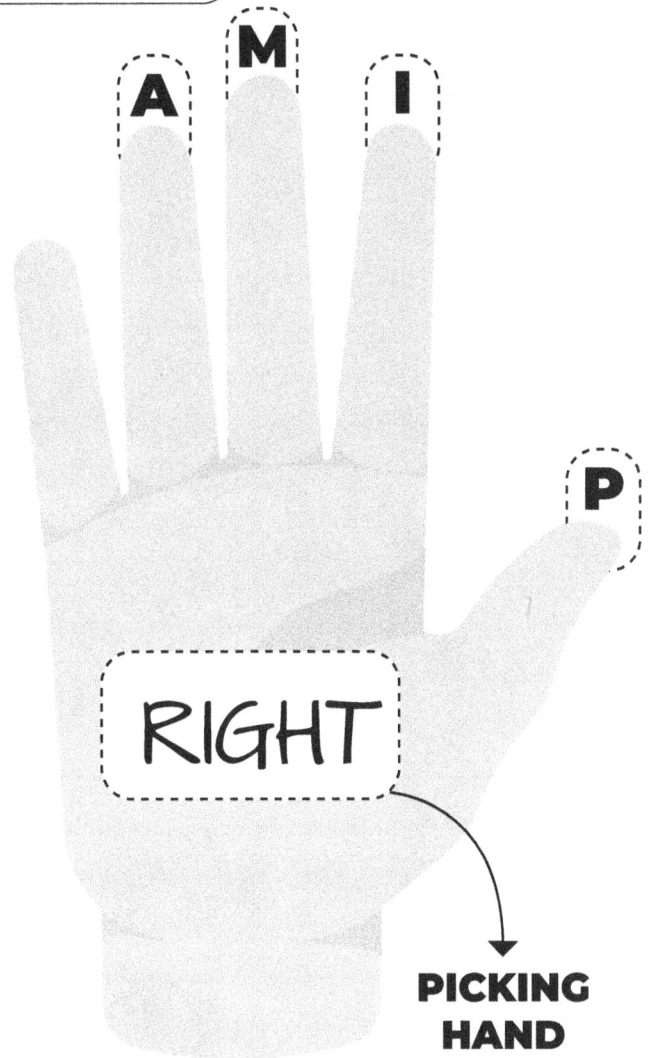

1   2   3   4

A   M   I   P

LEFT

RIGHT

FRETTING HAND

PICKING HAND

NOTES ON THE UKULELE NECK

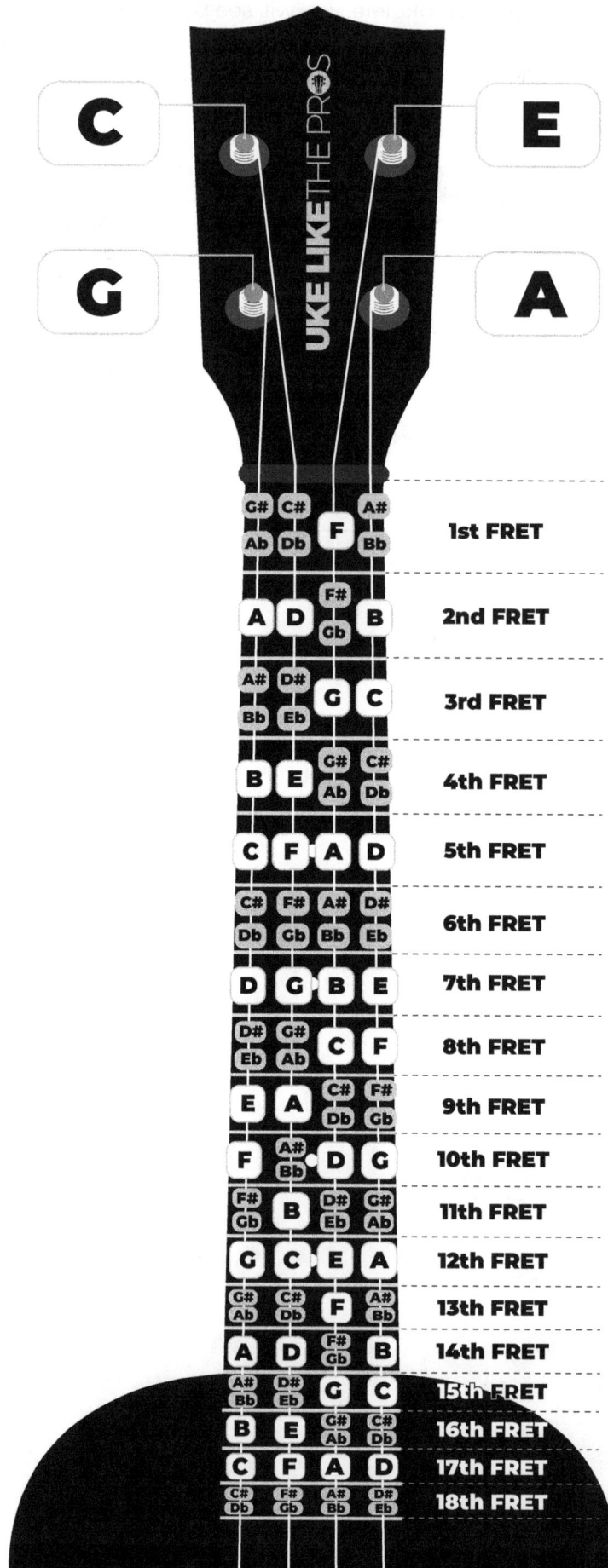

C   E

G   A

UKE LIKE THE PROS

Fret	String 1	String 2	String 3	String 4
1st FRET	G#/Ab	C#/Db	F	A#/Bb
2nd FRET	A	D	F#/Gb	B
3rd FRET	A#/Bb	D#/Eb	G	C
4th FRET	B	E	G#/Ab	C#/Db
5th FRET	C	F	A	D
6th FRET	C#/Db	F#/Gb	A#/Bb	D#/Eb
7th FRET	D	G	B	E
8th FRET	D#/Eb	G#/Ab	C	F
9th FRET	E	A	C#/Db	F#/Gb
10th FRET	F	A#/Bb	D	G
11th FRET	F#/Gb	B	D#/Eb	G#/Ab
12th FRET	G	C	E	A
13th FRET	G#/Ab	C#/Db	F	A#/Bb
14th FRET	A	D	F#/Gb	B
15th FRET	A#/Bb	D#/Eb	G	C
16th FRET	B	E	G#/Ab	C#/Db
17th FRET	C	F	A	D
18th FRET	C#/Db	F#/Gb	A#/Bb	D#/Eb

UNDERSTANDING CHORD DIAGRAMS

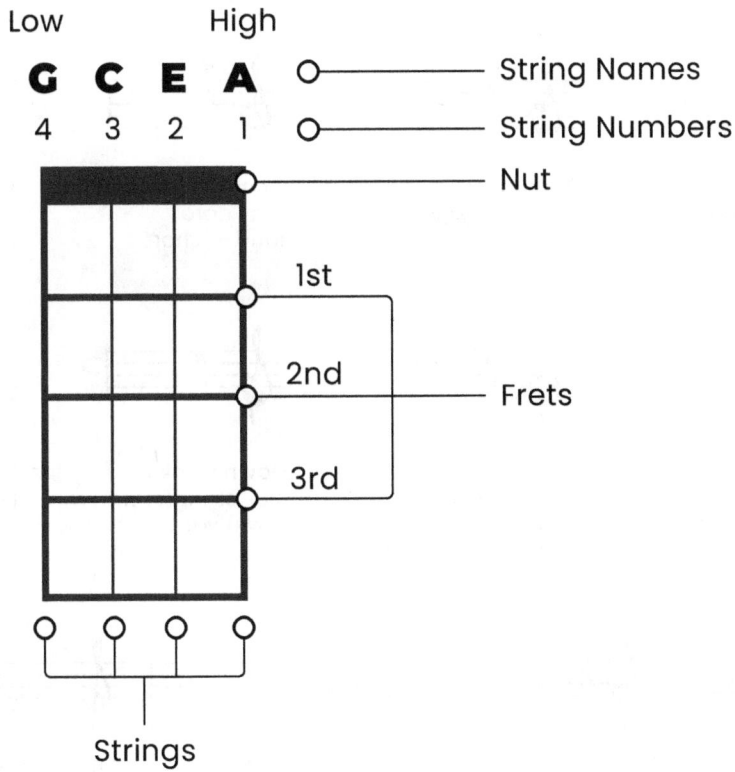

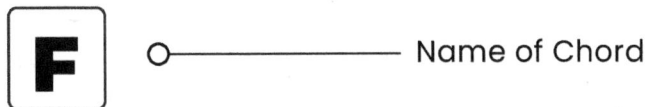

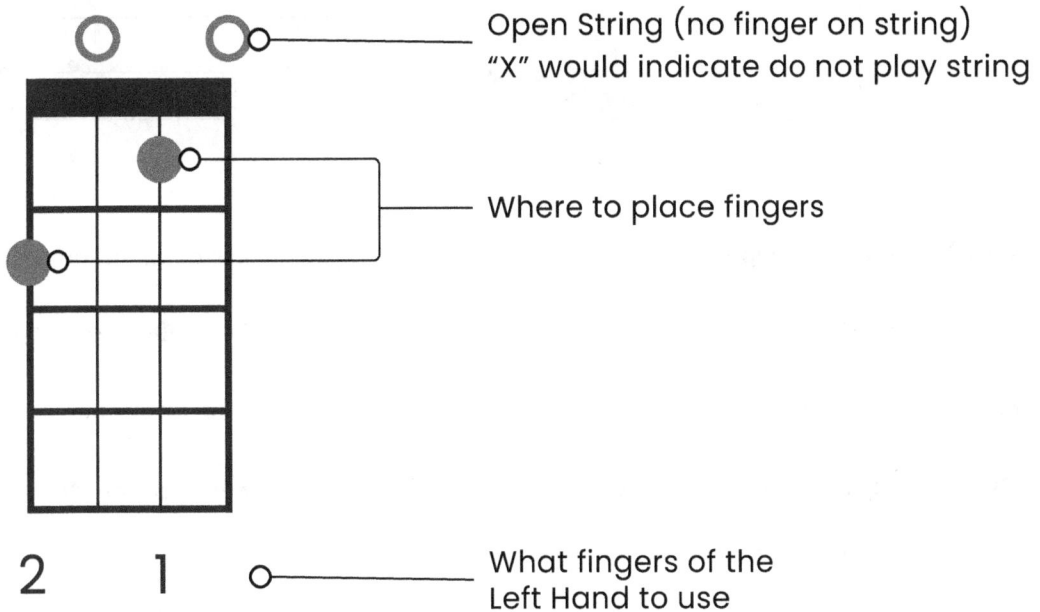

Low   High

G C E A — String Names

4   3   2   1 — String Numbers

— Nut

1st

2nd — Frets

3rd

Strings

F — Name of Chord

— Open String (no finger on string)
"X" would indicate do not play string

— Where to place fingers

2   1 — What fingers of the
Left Hand to use

F

MUSIC SYMBOLS TO KNOW

A variety of symbols, articulations, repeats, hammer on's, pull off's, bends, and slides.

Fermata:
Hold note

Staccato:
Play note short

Accent:
Play note loud

Accented Staccato:
Play note
loud + short

Vibrato
Rapid "shaking"
of note

Arpeggiated Chord:
Play the notes in fast
succession from low
to high strings

Grace Note:
Fast embellishment
note played before
the main note

Mute:
"Muffle" sound of
strings either with
left or right hand

Down Stroke:
Pick string(s) with a
downward motion

Up Stroke:
Pick string(s) with
an upward motion

Tie:
Play first note but
do not play second
note that it is tied to

Ledger Lines:
Extend the staff
higher or lower.

Slash Notation:
Repeat notes & rhythms
from previous measure

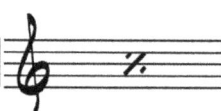

1 Bar Repeat:
Repeat notes &
rhythms from
previous measure

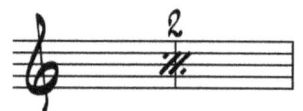

2 Bar Repeat:
Repeat notes & rhythms
from previous 2 measures

Repeat Sign:
(Beginning)

Repeat Sign:
(End)

1st Ending:
Play this part the
first time only

2nd Ending:
Play this part
the second time

(D.C. AL FINE) – *D.C.* (da capo) means go to the beginning of the tune and stop when you get to *Fine*

(D.C. AL CODA) – *D.C.* means go to the beginning of the tune and jump to *Coda* ⊕ when you see the sign ⊕

(D.S. AL FINE) – *D.S.* (dal segno) means go to the *Sign* 𝄋 and stop when you get to *Fine*

(D.S. AL CODA) – *D.S.* means go to the *Sign* 𝄋 And Jump to the *Coda* ⊕ when you see ⊕

SIM... – Play the same rhythm, strum pattern, or picking pattern as the previous measure

ETC... – Continue the same rhythm, strum pattern, or picking pattern as the previous measure

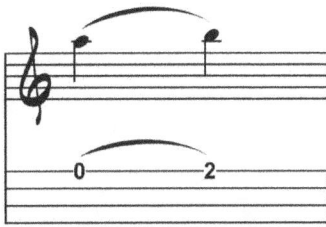

Hammer On:
Pick first note then hammer on to the next note without picking it.

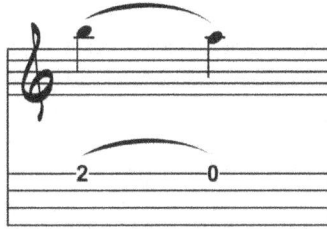

Pull Off:
Pick first note then pull off to the next note without picking it.

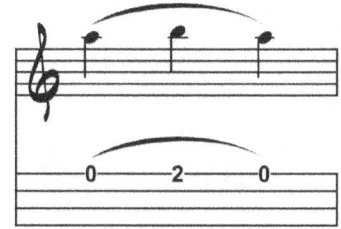

Hammer On & Pull Off:
Pick first note, hammer on to the next note, and pull off to the last note all in one motion.

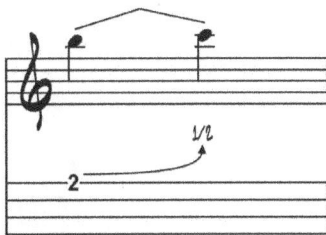

1/2 Step Bend:
Bend the first note a 1/2 step or 1 fret.

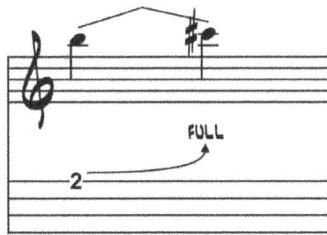

Whole Step Bend:
Bend the first note a whole step or 2 frets.

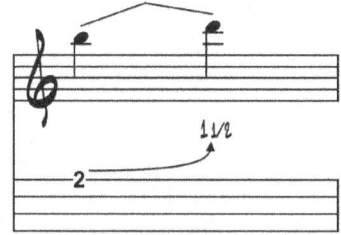

Step & 1/2 Bend:
Bend the first note 1 1/2 steps or 3 frets.

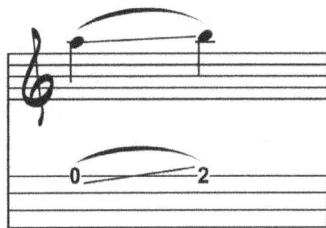

Forward Slide:
Pick first note and slide up to higher note.

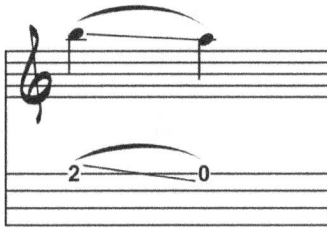

Backward Slide:
Pick first note and slide back to lower note.

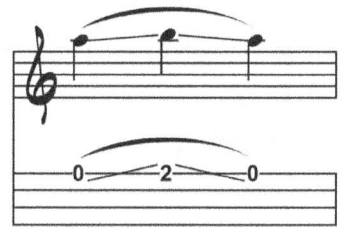

Forward/Backward Slide:
Pick first note, slide up to next note and then slide back.

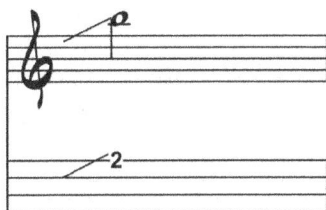

Slide Into Note:
Slide from 2-3 frets below note.

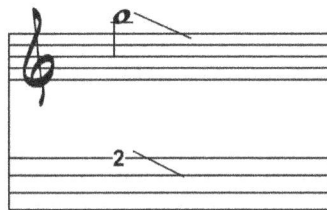

Slide Off Note:
Slide off 2-5 frets after note.

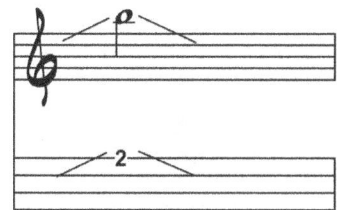

Slide Into Note then Slide Off Note.

H

CHORD CHART

These are some of the most widely used chords in all of music. Although there are more chords that are listed, these chords represent the most widely used shapes.

MAJOR CHORDS

A	B	C	D	E	F	G
2 1	3 2 1 1	3	1 1 2	2 2 3 1	2 1	1 3 2

MINOR CHORDS

A min	B min	C min	D min	E min	F min	G min
2	3 1 1 1	3 1 1 1	2 3 1	3 2 1	3 4 2 1	2 3 1

B min: 2nd FRET
C min: 3rd FRET
E min: 2nd FRET
F min: 3rd FRET

DOMINANT 7th CHORDS

A⁷	B⁷	C⁷	D⁷	E⁷	F⁷	G⁷
1	3 2 1	1	2 3	1 2 3	2 3 1 4	2 1 3

I

MAJOR 7th CHORDS

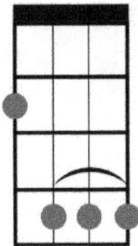
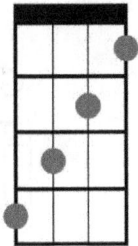
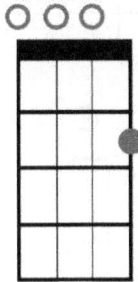
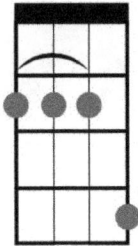
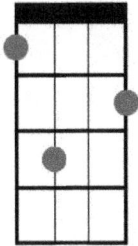
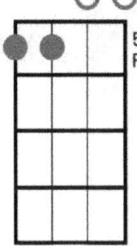
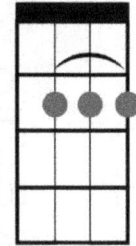

MINOR 7th CHORDS

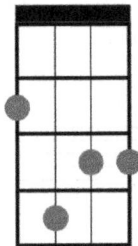
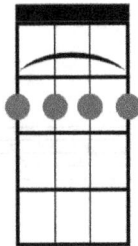
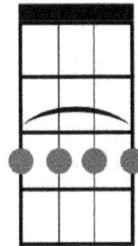
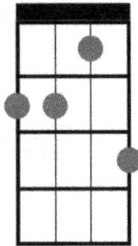
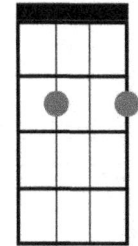
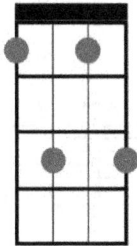
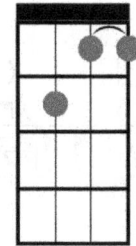

SUS + ADD CHORDS

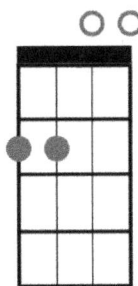
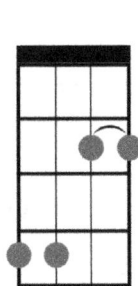
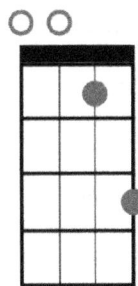
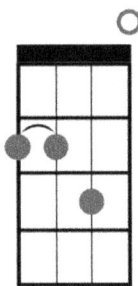
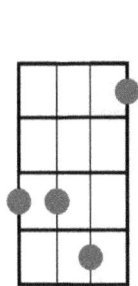
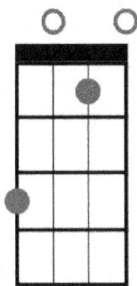
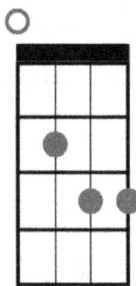

BEGINNING STRUM PATTERNS

These 4 rhythms, the whole note (rings for 4 beats), the half note (rings for 2 beats), the quarter note (rings for 1 beat), and the eighth note (rings for ½ a beat) make up the most important strum patterns for ukulele. Study and memorize these rhythms and strum patterns.

ADVANCED STRUM PATTERNS

This takes the 4 main rhythms (whole note, half note, quarter note, and eighth note) and adds the sixteenth note (rings out for ¼ of a beat) to the mix. You can get up to 4 sixteenth notes in a beat, and these strum patterns will give you a contemporary sound to your playing and strumming. Use the counting provided to lock in each strum pattern.

ABOUT THE AUTHOR

Terry Carter is a San Diego-based ukulele player, surfer, songwriter, and creator of ukelikethepros.com, rock-likethepros.com and terrycartermusicstore.com. With over 25 years as a professional musician, educator and Los Angeles studio musician, Terry has worked with greats like Weezer, Josh Groban, Robby Krieger (The Doors), 2-time Grammy winning composer Christopher Tin (Calling All Dawns), Duff McKagan (Guns N' Roses), Grammy winning producer Charles Goodan (Santana/ Rolling Stones), and the Los Angeles Philharmonic. Terry has written and produced tracks for commercials (Discount Tire and Puma) and TV shows, including Scorpion (CBS), Pit Bulls & Parolees (Animal Planet), Trippin', Wildboyz, and The Real World (MTV). He has self-published over 25 books for Uke Like The Pros and Rock Like The Pros, filmed over 30 ukulele and guitar online courses, and has tens of millions of views on his docial media channels.

Terry received a Master of Music in Studio/Jazz Guitar Performance from University of Southern California and a Bachelor of Music from San Diego State University, with an emphasis in Jazz Studies and Music Education. He has taught at the University of Southern California, San Diego State University, Santa Monica College, Miracosta College, and Los Angeles Trade Tech College.

TERRY CARTER MUSIC STORE

All your music needs at the #1 music store, **terrycartermusicstore.com**

Baritones

Ukuleles

Guitars

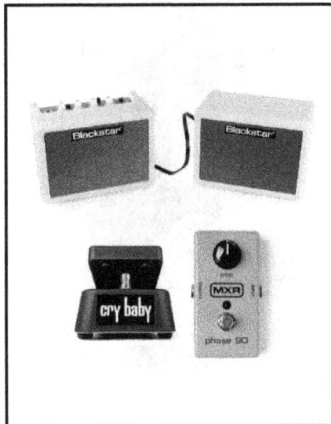

Amplifiers and
Pedals

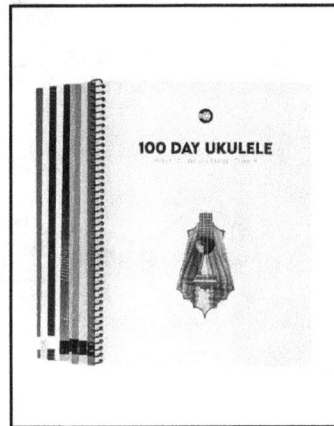

Books

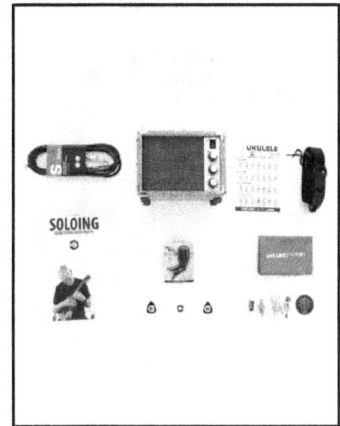

Accessories

N

ONLINE UKULELE COURSES

The perfect place to learn how to play Ukulele, Baritone Ukulele, Guitar and Guitarlele.

ULTP Roadmap
WHERE TO START?

1) UKULELE BEGINNER
A. Beginning Ukulele Starter Course
B. Beginning Ukulele Bootcamp Course
C. Ukulele Fundamentals Course
D. Ukulele Practice & Technique Course
E. Master the Ukulele 1

2) UKULELE INTERMEDIATE
A. Master The Ukulele 2
B. Beginning Music Reading
C. 23 Ultimate Chord Progressions
D. Beginning Ukulele Fingerstyle Course

3) UKULELE ADVANCED
A. Ukulele Blues Mastery Course
B. Beginning Ukulele Soloing Course
C. Fingerstyle Mastery Course
D. Jazz Swing Mastery Course

MORE OPTIONS!

FUNLAND
A. Beginning Ukulele Kids Course Songbook
B. 21 Popular Songs for Ukulele
C. The Best Ukulele Christmas Songs
D. 10 Classic Rock Licks
E. Guitar Fundamentals

BARITONE UKULELE
A. Beginning Baritone Ukulele Bootcamp Course
B. 6 Weeks Baritone Q&A
C. Baritone Blues Mastery Course
D. Beginning Baritone Fingerstyle Course

GUITARLELE
A. Guitarlele Starter Course
B. 6 Weeks Guitarlele Q&A
C. Guitarlele Course for Ukulele and Guitar Players
D. Guitarlele Blues Mastery Course

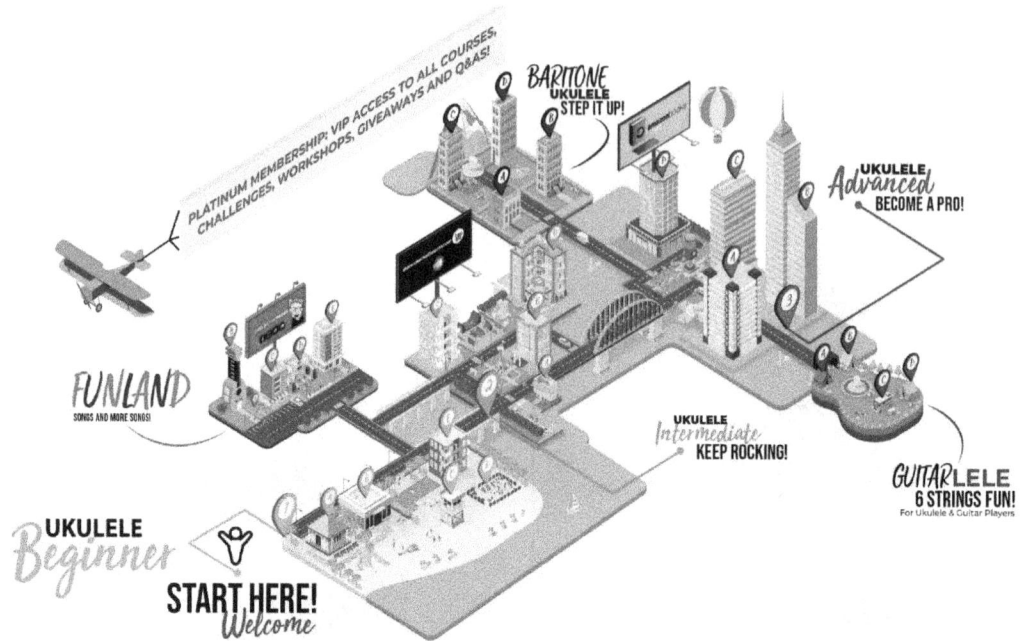

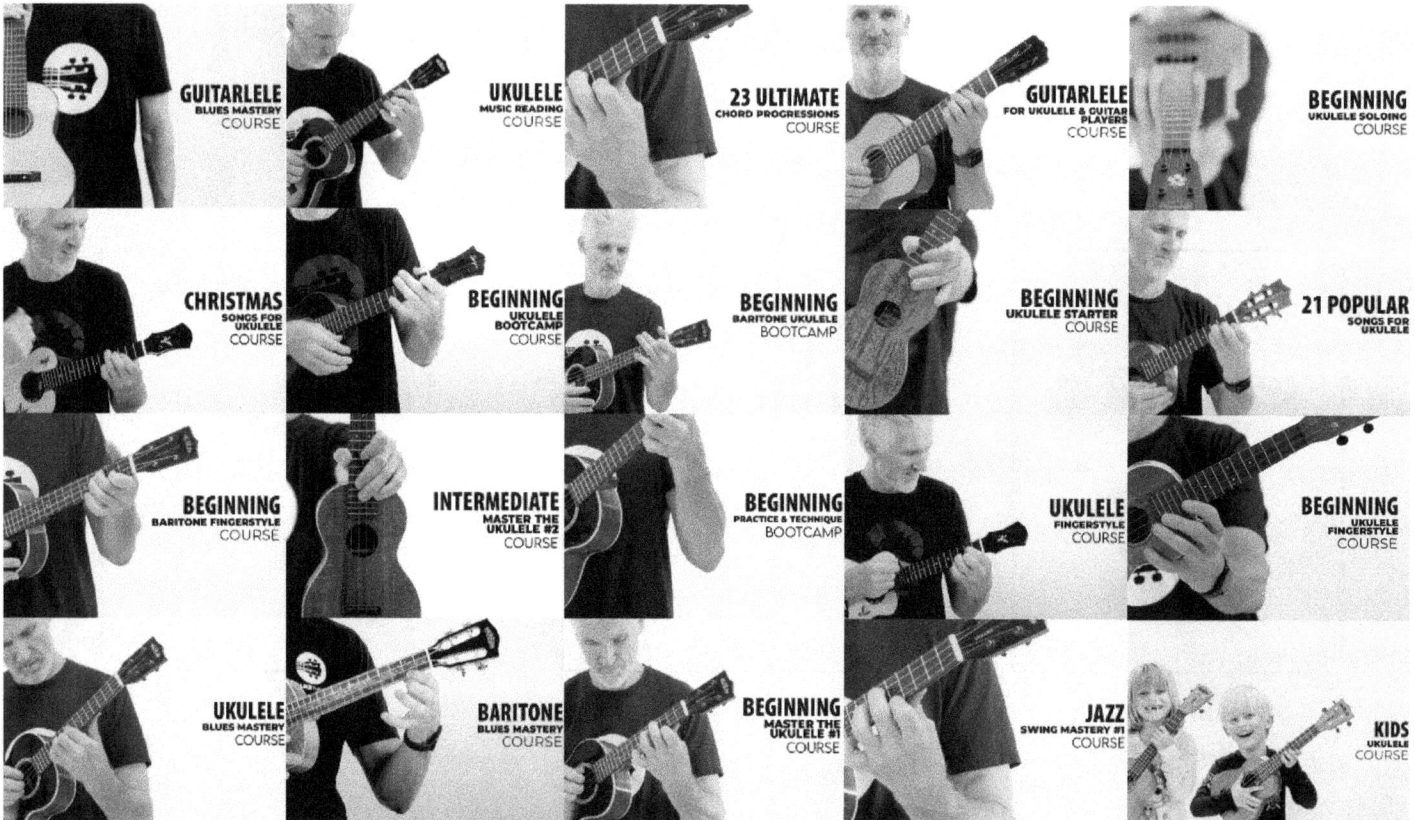

PLATINUM MEMBERSHIP: VIP ACCESS TO ALL COURSES, CHALLENGES, WORKSHOPS, GIVEAWAYS AND Q&AS!

BARITONE UKULELE STEP IT UP!

UKULELE *Advanced* BECOME A PRO!

FUNLAND SONGS AND MORE SONGS!

UKULELE *Intermediate* KEEP ROCKING!

GUITARLELE 6 STRINGS FUN! For Ukulele & Guitar Players

UKULELE *Beginner*

START HERE! *Welcome*

GUITARLELE BLUES MASTERY COURSE

UKULELE MUSIC READING COURSE

23 ULTIMATE CHORD PROGRESSIONS COURSE

GUITARLELE FOR UKULELE & GUITAR PLAYERS COURSE

BEGINNING UKULELE SOLOING COURSE

CHRISTMAS SONGS FOR UKULELE COURSE

BEGINNING UKULELE BOOTCAMP COURSE

BEGINNING BARITONE UKULELE BOOTCAMP

BEGINNING UKULELE STARTER COURSE

21 POPULAR SONGS FOR UKULELE

BEGINNING BARITONE FINGERSTYLE COURSE

INTERMEDIATE MASTER THE UKULELE #2 COURSE

BEGINNING PRACTICE & TECHNIQUE BOOTCAMP

UKULELE FINGERSTYLE COURSE

BEGINNING UKULELE FINGERSTYLE COURSE

UKULELE BLUES MASTERY COURSE

BARITONE BLUES MASTERY COURSE

BEGINNING MASTER THE UKULELE #1 COURSE

JAZZ SWING MASTERY #1 COURSE

KIDS UKULELE COURSE

Courses For All Levels
UKELIKETHEPROS.COM

UKELIKETHEPROS.COM
BLOG.UKELIKETHEPROS.COM
TERRYCARTERMUSICSTORE.COM
BUYSTRINGSONLINE.COM

@ukelikethepros

INTERESTED IN GUITAR CONTENT?
ROCKLIKETHEPROS.COM